SIC

Childrens Book

Table of Contents

INTRODUCTION

HOW TO USE THIS MANUAL

If you want your child to be able to speak with confidence, assurance, and with a voice that is heard clearly and easily understood, then this manual is for you.

The comprehensive format and content will instruct your children, through exercises, to work towards clear speech and a voice that has a pleasant listening quality when speaking in conversation, to an audience reciting poems, or taking part in dramatic pieces.

What to do - Choose a couple of exercises each from the Relaxation and Posture Chapters, then choose one other chapter you want to focus on, for your child, when you find the time. You will only need ten minutes or so if you choose this method, so it might be a good time while having breakfast, straight after school, in the car on the way to/from school, or just before bed. To keep the exercises fresh for your children, choose one or two new exercises from each chapter, each time you practice.

CHAPTER ONE –RELAXATION

The first part of every speech or drama lesson is getting your child relaxed. Relaxation in terms of speech doesn't mean ready to fall asleep, it is simply adjusting small parts of our body to ensure we can breathe properly and produce the best speaking voice we can. If there is undue tension in any muscles that are used for breathing or voice production then the speech produced will have some fault, for example, a hard tone or harsh breathing. The outcome of the speech produced will not be as effective, or as clear, as it could be.

If we are too tense we cannot think clearly, and what we want to say may come out all jumbled and senseless. Being tense means we cannot control our voice and make it sound the way we want. This can be very detrimental, especially if we are going to speak in public, or convince someone about something.

Some reasons why we may feel tension:

- We worry that the listener may not like what we have to say
- We might be concerned that what we have to say isn't suitable for the audience
- We're not sure what the words that we're saying mean
- We're not sure that we can express our ideas clearly
- We might be worried that we're going to forget our memorised work
- We are worried that we won't be loud enough for everyone to hear

Some signs of tension can be:

- Screwing your hands into tight balls
- Shoulders pulling up close to the ears
- Jiggling from foot to foot, or shaking a leg or arm
- Breathing in noisily through the mouth
- Over gesturing

- Saying um or ah

- Blinking rapidly

- Licking lips

A few simple exercises can help!

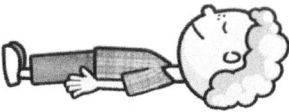

Part One: Visualisation and body relaxing

Have your child lie down and close their eyes. Tell them to keep your thoughts in their head. Always start with breathing in through the nose and out through the mouth, three times at normal speed.

1. Now breathe deeper into the lungs imagining the air you are breathing is yellow, warm, bright yellow. Imagine the air is going all through your body, down

to the tips of your fingers and toes. When you breathe out, imagine the air is grey-black. All your negative thoughts of the day are leaving your body with that grey air. Breathe in yellow, fill up your entire body, and breathe out grey. Repeat three times.

2. Imagine you are lying on a cloud, a big, white, fluffy cloud, and this cloud is taking you for a trip along the sky. Imagine the warm breeze in your face (if you are in a hot climate, imagine a cool breeze). Relax into your cloud because it can hold you up without any effort. Relax into your cloud as it carries you over the beautiful blue skies. Imagine the cloud getting faster and faster as it swoops and dives across the sky. It's fun! You are loving it! The cloud is holding you up, the breeze is on your face, and you feel secure and happy.

3. Lie on your back, hands by your sides. Tense up all your muscles and squeeze really tight. Hold onto all those squeezed muscles while you count to three and then suddenly relax them all at the same time. Do this two or three times. Then just tense up one part of your body at a time, starting with your toes, then your foot, then ankle, calf, knees, thighs, squeeze your bottom and tummy, chest, arms all the way down to your finger, neck muscles, and your whole head. Hold all muscles tensed for a count of one, two, three, then relax.

4. Curl up into a little ball then spring up like a jack-in-the-box, then flop back down into a ball. Repeat twice more, then on the last one don't flop down but walk around like a tin soldier, with stiff arms and legs, then flop down and stay on the floor. Slowly curl up onto your side and push yourself up to sitting. Sit on your knees, hands in front of you, then push yourself up to standing with feet on the ground, knees bent and hands on the floor. Take your hands off the floor as you push yourself up to standing.

5. Lie on the floor and make yourself as long as possible - imagine you are a piece of elastic and someone is pulling you, then they let go. Repeat this several times.

   Stand up and stretch your arms up over your head, trying to reach the roof. Hold this position for two seconds, then allow your body to break at the waist, so your arms should flop down and your head hang free between your arms (bend your knees slightly as you do this). Very slowly, start pulling yourself up into standing position again. Your hands should hang freely by your sides as you stand tall.

6. While you are standing with your feet hip width apart, hold your arms out in front of you at a 90 degree angle from your body. Imagine you are pushing hard up

against a wall. Push while you count to five, then relax your arms to your sides. Repeat once more.

7. In the same standing position as number 7, let your head fall so your chin is on your chest. Raise it slowly until it feels like your head is balanced between your shoulders. Repeat this, but imagine your head is getting heavier as it falls and lighter as you bring it back up. Do the same again, but let your head fall backwards and bring it forwards without any effort. Now look over your right shoulder as far as you can and slowly bring it back to the centre. Look over your left shoulder and bring it back to the centre.

NOTE: YOUR HEAD AND NECK ARE NOT A BALL IN SOCKET LIKE YOUR ARMS AND SHOULDERS, SO DO NOT ROTATE YOUR HEAD AROUND IN A CIRCLE AS THIS MAY CAUSE DAMAGE. IF YOU HAVE ANY PAIN IN YOUR HEAD OR NECK BEFORE YOU DO THESE EXERCISES, SEE YOUR DOCTOR FIRST.

8. Stretch your arms out to the sides as far as they can go. Hold this position, then drop your arms to your sides. Do this three times, then raise your shoulders to get them as close to your ears as possible. Drop them down. Repeat three times also.

9. Push your shoulders forward and try to get them to meet in the middle, then relax them quickly so they drop to normal position easily. Repeat this three

times. Now, do the same but this time pull your shoulders back, as if to meet at the spine. Repeat three times.

10. Lift your chest up and out as if you are a soldier on parade. Let it drop back then do this again three more times.

Part Two – Face relaxation

1. Try to move your hair forwards and backwards.

2. Wriggle your ears.

3. Twitch your nose.

4. Move your eyebrows up and down as fast as you can, move one of your eyebrows up and down at a time.

5. Pretend to chew a large piece of chewing gum. Now pretend you have a very small piece of chewing gum and chew that rapidly.

6. Count your teeth with your tongue, try to touch your nose with your tongue, now touch your chin with your tongue. See if your tongue can touch the right ear, now the left.

7. Screw up your face as tight as you can, then relax, smile as hard as you can, then relax.

8. Pretend to cry, then laugh!

9. Open your eyes wide and try to keep them like that while you continue with more exercises.

Part Three – Voice relaxation

Voice relaxation is essential for good speaking. Many people trap their voice at the back of their throat (this is something we will explore later in the chapter in relation to pitch and tone) and this can give the effect of the words being swallowed down, as opposed to coming out of the mouth clearly. When this fault occurs, their throat and jaw are usually very tense giving the voice an almost tight sound. You cannot produce clear, resonant tone when you have tension anywhere in your throat, jaw, lips, tongue, hard and soft palate.

Following are some exercises to help relax those areas to help produce a beautiful voice - choose one or two to practise every day after your posture and visualisation exercises.

1. Yawn. Open up your mouth really wide, breathe in while trying to keep your shoulders down. Breathe out of your yawn with a full-size 'ahhhh' sound. Do this again, finishing with a big 'hummm'.

2. Keep your lips closed but drop your jaw as far as it will go without opening your lips.

3. Say these words in an exaggerated way, really dropping your jaw and keeping your mouth wide - father, car, barn, hang, lone, fast, farms, past.

4. Say these sentences two or three times over - yellow yo-yos/red leather yellow leather/will you wait for Will/pass the pencils please/blow up the big blue balloon.

If you are going to be speaking in public, or you are nervous for any reason about speaking to others, choose your favourite exercises from visualisation and voice relaxation and practice frequently before the event. Even minutes before giving the speech or making that phone call...it will help!

Homework:

Choose 2 or 3 exercises from each section and write them in here. Then practice them every day.

CHAPTER TWO - POSTURE

Poor posture can be one of the underlying reasons for poor quality of speech because it can really affect voice and breathing, which are two elements that are crucial for clear speech. If our posture is incorrect our lungs cannot expand properly, we can't breathe properly and we can't produce clear speech. Poor posture can also cause undue tension in an area like your throat, which can affect the quality of your voice.

Before you continue with any other speech exercises, start with a few postural exercises with your child. These are very simple exercises that you should encourage daily, at the start of every 'clear speech' lesson.

POOR POSTURE

Usually, poor posture is due to bad habits, but if you have concerns about your posture, or your child's posture, because of a medical condition, see your doctor before you start any of these exercises.

Our posture changes hugely as we age. If we watch a toddler we can see how they move with grace and poise, but we can soon see that their posture starts to degenerate around the age of five or six, just when we start school. Many factors of everyday life can affect our posture, most of which include some sort of stress, tension or prolonged activity in one place. For example, sitting for long periods of time, leaning over the desk to write, carting around very heavy bags full of books or laptops.

We actually place more stress on our back when we sit, so the exercises include sitting in a way that supports our spine. As we usually slump back when we sit, it's a good idea to have seats that have backs that slope forwards, to help stop this slumping.

We need to be very aware of our posture and exercise daily, and really all day, to keep our posture at its best.

SOME COMMON FAULTS

1. Slumping shoulders down towards the abdomen so the spine is rounded, which will affect breathing.
2. Rounding the shoulders so they stick forward and cause tension in the neck.
3. Pushing the trunk of your body too far forward and up - like standing to attention in the army. This also affects breathing.
4. Pulling your shoulders up around your ears, like you've just been given a fright. This will produce tension in the throat and affect your voice.
5. Leaning back and putting all your weight on your heels. This will cause you to tense up your abdomen so breathing will require extra work.

EXERCISES TO HELP CORRECT OUR POSTURE

Simply becoming aware of how we stand, sit and walk throughout the day can be a big help towards correcting our posture. Following are some exercises to start with, before continuing with your other speech exercises.

1. Stand with feet hip width apart, arms hanging loosely at your sides. Come up onto your tip toes and slowly lower your heel, so your weight is evenly balanced on three points - the ball of your foot underneath your big toe, the ball of your foot underneath your little toe, and your heel.

2. Put a finger on top of your head and push your head up against your finger. Pull your tummy button in towards your back. Take your finger away but keep standing straight and tummy pulled in.

3. Bend slowly down from the waist and swing your arms loosely so they are either touching the floor or close to it. Imagine you are a puppet on a string and the puppeteer is slowly pulling you up, one vertebra at a time, until your head is back up on your shoulders. Repeat exercises two and three.

4. The most well-known posture exercise of all... Place a smallish, hard covered book on your head. Balance it and walk around the room. Have a conversation with someone, making sure your book stays on your head. Time yourself to see how long it can stay on. Have competitions with friends or family - who is the best?

5. Put a straight backed chair in front of the mirror. Sit on the seat making sure you can feel both your sitting bones on your bottom as you sit, feet on the floor with weight on the three points from exercise one. Repeat exercise two, but in sitting position. Note - try to maintain this when you sit at school or work.

6. Practise picking up an object off the floor by squatting down.

Don't forget, practise these exercises every day, just choose one or two first thing in the morning and remind yourself throughout the day to sit or stand correctly.

CHAPTER THREE – BREATHING

We breathe, really, without giving it much thought. We involuntarily use some muscles that cause us to breathe without our deliberate control. However, breath is the 'motor power' of the voice and it needs to be a steady, controlled flow.

Good breath control is only achieved by developing the accepted, correct method of breathing, which is the basis of good, effective voice production. Faulty methods lead to tension in various muscles, lack of resonance and weak projection.

If we want to use our voices effectively, we need to learn how to control our breathing for our benefit. We need to know the correct process of breathing.

Technical bit – The correct process of breathing is 'intercostal diaphragmatic', simply meaning to use the diaphragm along with muscles controlling the ribs, known as the inner and outer costal muscles, which are short and extend between the ribs, for breathing. The whole process of breathing is called respiration.

This is what happens when we breathe

Firstly, you use your rib muscles to start expanding your ribs out and up before you take a breath. When you inhale air, through the nose or mouth, it travels down the pharynx, then through the larynx, then trachea in the bronchial tubes, then finally into the lungs. At the same time, the diaphragm, a large, umbrella shaped muscle, descends about 10cm, and the ribs (which the intercostal muscles expand) lift out and up to allow more capacity in the lungs (you need ample capacity for speaking). We then exhale and the abdominal muscle (a muscle which serves as a floor for the diaphragm and a roof for the abdomen) pushes the diaphragm back to its normal position (known as abdominal press) and the ribs resume their normal position. These two movements together push the air steadily out of the lungs, up the trachea, through the larynx, pharynx, and back out the nose or mouth.

It is important that the expiration of air is steady, smooth and controlled for good voice production.

This method ensures complete control over the outgoing breath and good breath power. Of course, you need exercises and practice to gain the control required for really effective speech. To make sure you are using the correct method of breathing, you need to make sure of the following signs:

- Chin is sitting in correct position
- Shoulders straight
- Normal back
- Good balance

Note - you will find this information in the 'Posture' chapter.

There are many faulty methods of breathing, such as:

1. Shallow breathing (or clavicular). This is when only the top section of the lungs are filled with air. This happens quite naturally when you undertake some forms of exercise, like cycling or running. This causes tightening of the throat and chest muscles and can lead to injury of the voice.

   Signs that this method is being used:

   - Drawn in chin
   - Harsh voice

- Stiff and protruding chest

- Shoulders moving up and down

- Hollow back

- Weight on toes

2. Abdominal breathing. In this type of breathing the ribs are not expanded and the air is only taken into the base of the lungs. Because the ribs are not fully used, the outgoing air is uncontrolled and the result is breathiness. Visible signs include:

- Breathy voice

- Undeveloped chest

- Forward shoulders

- Rounded back

- Protruding abdomen

- Weight on heels

There is also noisy breathing, when someone sucks air in through partly closed teeth, or, if there's tension in the throat it will constrict and block air. If a speaker runs out of breath while speaking they may not have enough control over their breathing muscles. Once again, with weak breathing muscles a speaker may find they are not loud enough to be heard, or they start loud but trail off at the end. This is due to lack of control and capacity, so it is very important to practise breathing exercises (after relaxation and posture) every day.

The following are exercises that are to follow on from relaxation and posture. Choose half a dozen new ones EVERY DAY. If you feel faint while you are doing any breathing exercises, it's time to take a break and breathe regularly. All these exercises should be in standing position unless otherwise stated. When you are standing, make sure your posture is correct - see the "Posture" chapter for details on this.

1. Pretend you are breathing in the scent of a flower. Hold on to the flower, bring the flower to your nose and (keeping your shoulders level) take a deep breath in through your nose, until your lungs are completely filled up. Hold your breath for the count of 1,2,3 and slowly let your breath out through your mouth.

2. Pretend you have a candle in your hand, blow with three short puffs – wh, wh, wh. Now one long puff, whuh....

3. Hold up all ten fingers about 20cm from your face. Spread your fingers out and aim breath at each finger as if blowing out a candle.

4. Very gently blow up a balloon. Blow up a paper bag and burst it.

5. Pretend there is a birthday cake in front of you with fifty candles on it. Breathe in through your nose and blow them all at once. Try again blowing one out at a time.

6. Use straws to blow table tennis balls across a table.

7. Using your breath, keep a feather or leaf hovering in the air.

8. Pretend there is a heavy ball in front of you. Bend to pick it up and as you do, start to breathe in. Keep inhaling as you lift the heavy ball up over your head. Hold it there and then as you throw it down, drop the ball in front of you with a loud 'Hahhhh'

9. Hold your hands in front of your body, so your arms look like a circle, in front of your tummy button. Raise them up and out until they are stretched over your head. Breathe in while you do this. With arms in the air, hold for the count of 3. Bring your arms down as you slowly release the rest of your breath.

10. Take a deep breath in, slowly through your nose. Laugh a big, loud HA, HA, HA and exhale the rest of your breath. Do this twice.

11. Take a deep breath in, slowly through your nose. Close your lips and laugh soundlessly through your nose.

12. Take a breath through your nose and, as you exhale, count from one to five on that single breath. Do it again, but this time count from one to ten. Next time, count one to fifteen, then one to twenty. Keep doing this exercise, seeing who can go the furthest. This exercise must be done without strain.

13. Lie down and place a book on your tummy just where your ribs are. Relax your body and flatten your tummy as much as you can. As you breathe in, the book will rise, when you breathe out it will go back down.

14. Put your hand on the lower part of your ribs and press firmly. Breathe in against your hands to the count of three. Keep your hands in place and breathe out to a slow count of nine.

15. Place your hand about 10cm in front of your mouth. Take a breath in through your nose with enough breath for you to say the alphabet. Start speaking the alphabet as you gradually move your arm away. Think of placing each letter in the palm of your hand.

16. Breathe in through your nose and breathe out whispering the 'OO' sound. Do it again but with an 'EE' sound.

17. Same as number 16, but on the exhale make the make the 'OO' sound quiet the 'EE' sound loud.

18. Same as number 16 and 17, but speak loudly and fast the "OO' sound, then let the rest of the air out with a long 'AH' sound.

19. Stand with your arms loose at your sides. Move them up to shoulder height horizontally and then, as you breathe in to the count of five, raise them to join in the middle above your head. Count to three in your head and bring your arms back down to your sides to the count of ten.

20. Say the alphabet in one breath. Stop if you are straining your voice but keep practicing this exercise until you can easily say the alphabet on one breath.

CHAPTER FOUR – VOICE PRODUCTION

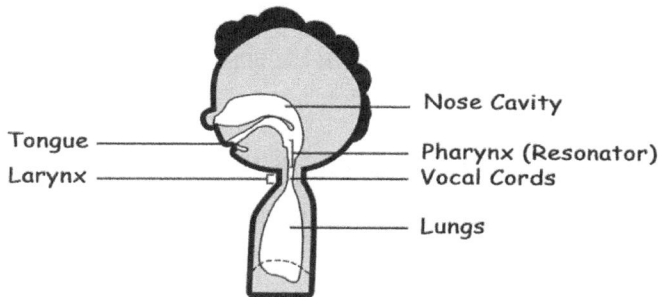

The voice is amplified by the resonators and speech is formed by the articulative organs.

In the following chapters we will be covering the following:

- Exercising our resonators so we can deliver a richer tone

- Exercising the organs of articulation to produce a clearer sound

- Working on pitch, pace and tone so our voice is not too high or low, and we can vary our pitch to create more interesting speech

- Finally, work on forward placement to direct your speech to a certain point

To make sure we have good voice production, it is necessary to have good control over outgoing breath, as well as to make sure we have a clear, resonant voice, good articulation and projection and to develop interesting delivery through good modulation.

We have covered how to gain good control over our breath in the previous chapters on relaxation, posture and breath control.

The following chapters will have various exercises to ensure you have developed all the necessary features for good voice production.

The most important point is that this is not just a one off. You must continue to practice these exercises throughout your LIFE!

We know how we breathe correctly and we can see how voice (or sound) is produced. We now have to continue through the chapters starting with RESONATION to go on with developing our beautiful speaking voice using more exercises.

CHAPTER FIVE – RESONANCE

The general function of the resonators is to produce tone.

The three main resonators are:

1. The back of your throat (pharynx-pharyngial resonance).

2. The hollows of your nose and cheeks (nasal resonance).

3. The mouth (oral cavity-oral resonance).

Less important resonators are the upper cavity of the chest, the larynx, and the forehead.

When a current of air is passed through a hollow space, a resonant pitch is heard. Each hollow space has its own resonant pitch, which depends on the size and number of its openings (orifices). If the initial sound is intensified in our resonating cavities, then a true balanced tone can be achieved.

To make sure the full resonance is achieved in the pharynx, it is necessary to see that there is no tension in the neck and the correct breathing method is used to make sure the passage is opened to its full extent. We have covered exercises in chapters one to three to make sure this is the case.

For nasal resonance, it is imperative that the soft palate and tongue are active so that they are capable of opening or closing the passage into the nose as required. It should be opened for the nasal sounds, M, N, NG, and closed for all other sounds.

For oral resonance, it is important that each vowel is formed with its own particular shaping, ensuring that the correct resonant pitch is achieved. The hollow space most actively concerned with vowel formation is the mouth. Each vowel possesses a note of a definite and distinctive pitch, which is the result of breathing out through the resonation cavities in this position. As each vowel has a different sound, then the mouth has a different shape and each also has a different resonant pitch. As we carry our accent in our vowel sounds, exercises for vowel formation will be covered in a following chapter.

Say these exercises one at a time to your children and get them to follow your instructions while you also take part with them. Choose as many, or as few, as you like, so if time is short then four in one session is fine.

The following exercises are for pharyngeal and nasal resonance.

1. Drop the jaw several times and say – Mah Mah Mah.

2. Say this really fast - ing, ing, ing, ing, ing.

3. Poke your tongue our as far as it will go. Let it lie still. Do this twice.

4. Say the word BOOM on a long breath. Feel the vibration in your lips, throat, cheeks, nose, forehead.

5. Open your mouth wide and breathe in through your nose and out though your mouth. Do this three times.

6. Hum 'Baa Baa Black Sheep' very gently. You should feel a tickling on your lips which should be very lightly pressed together with teeth slightly apart. Don't forget to stop to take a breath at the end of each line.

   • Baa Baa Black Sheep

- Have you any wool?
- Yes sir yes sir
- Three bags full
- One for the master
- One for the dame
- One for the little boy
- Who lives down the lane.

7. Face a wall and hum an 'M' continually. Step away from the wall but imagine leaving your 'M' sound at the wall.

8. Make an 'M' sound again, as if you have heard some good news. Repeat this five times with your voice getting louder.

9. Put your hands over your ears and say "good morning". Try to imagine the voice is outside of your head.

10. Whisper as you count up to ten slowly. Repeat, but this time say it as if you are a bell tolling for ten o'clock – so you will say it on one tone. Say it again, but out loud and clear as you normally would.

CHAPTER SIX - ARTICULATION
(VOWELS AND CONSONANTS)

There are 26 letters in the English alphabet but 44 sounds* in English. Articulation is taking those20 vowel and 24 consonant sounds and combining them into words.

Once the sound is resonated (practise in previous chapter) it is then formed into words (which are made up of vowels and consonants).

Words are formed by the articulative organs - teeth, tongue, lips, hard and soft palate (roof of mouth and back of throat). Each sound is produced by a definite position of one or other articulative organs, and if the shaping is not made properly, the sound produced will be inaccurate. We need to exercise our organs of articulation so we can produce a clear, clean, correct sound when we speak.

Vowels are formed mainly by the shape of the lips and the tongue. In some cases, we need to drop the jaw. For practise, we divide the tongue in to three positions - FRONT, CENTRE, BACK.

Say the following words so you can see where your tongue is positioned.

FRONT: Speed   Hid   Had

CENTRE: Hut   Hard   Heard

BACK: Hoot Hook Hawk Hock

Keep the tip of the tongue down when you practise vowels.

The quality of voice is heard through the formation of vowel sounds, so keep up the resonance practise to help work on quality, before your vowel practise.

We cover a lot of sounds in this chapter, so if time is short choose the sounds that you think need the most work.

*for video examples of how to say each 44 sound clearly in English go to www.sayitclearly.nz for online courses.

EXERCISES FOR VOWEL SOUNDS

The following poems are an excellent way to practise vowel sounds. There are 5 vowels in English but 14 different vowel sounds. These sounds are the most common. If you want to learn all 14 sounds you will find them, along with the 30 consonant sounds in the Masterclass - Excellence in English book (also available on Amazon). To see all the exercises in video go to www.sayitclearly.co.nz or Miriam McKenzie YouTube.

When you follow the instructions on the shape of your mouth when making certain sounds, have a look in a mirror so you can see what the shape looks like.

Repeat one of these poems every day to practise your vowel sounds.

AH

Open your mouth as if you were going to yawn. Every time this sound is in your speech relax your jaw and let the sound come forward.

- If we go down to the park
- When it is dark.
- We won't see very far
- Past the entry mark.

AW

Drop your jaw well down and bring the lips forward to make a soft round circle. Make sure the tip of your tongue is touching your lower teeth.

- There ought to be a law
- Against people who bore.
- It is like they were taught
- To talk like we are four.

OH

At the start of this sound drop your jaw and round your lips to make a large circle. Keep your teeth apart and tongue tip down. Make sure your lips are soft and not pulled tight.

- Rosa had a pony,
- Which she fed on burnt toast
- When her Mother told her "NO"
- Rosa and her pony would go.

OO

Put your index finger into your mouth and let your lips close softly over it. Now take out your finger leaving your lips in that shape. Make sure your teeth are the same distance apart as your lips, and tongue tip down.

- The cow says moo,
- A ghost goes boo.
- When you see a baby,
- You might gaa and goo.

Ŏ

Open your mouth nice and wide but keep lips soft and round in a small oval shape.

- Please be careful of the hot pot
- Make sure you don't drop

- It on to the table top.

OO

This is a short sound that can get caught in the back of your throat, so make sure you have done all your relaxation exercises, especially around your neck area, and section two of this chapter.

Make your lips into a shape like you were going to say 'moon', but don't push your lips out so far and drop your jaw a little more to make it easier for the sound to come out. Say 'good' for practise to see how it looks in the mirror (as compared to moon) and how it feels. Listen to my audio for the difference between this sound getting caught in the back of the throat, and letting it come out of the mouth.

- "That was good but you could
- Try harder next time."
- "Look, look see your book?
- You should put it on the hook."

EE

If you do this properly it will really soften the strong kiwi EE sound. Keep your teeth slightly open and don't pull your lips to each side like a smile. When you make this sound your lips will stay in a soft oval shape. The sides of your tongue will touch your top teeth but the tip will stay down AND the back of your tongue will also stay down!! Practise by putting your tongue into position and breathe heavily through the gap your tongue has created. If the back of your tongue doesn't stay down the tone will become hard, which is another trait of our Kiwi accent.

Practise these words - Meet, Meat, Key, Seal, Ceiling, Receive, Feel, Squeal, Teeth, Sweet, Teacher, Speak, Seems, Mean, Been.

Space between your teeth, lips oval shape and soft, tip of tongue behind lower teeth, rest of tongue flat. Send the sound out of your mouth, don't let the back of your tongue up or else the sound will catch at the back of your throat. Keep lips oval – don't pull them back.

- Quick, come over here
- Quick, bring a drink
- Quick, don't spill the drink
- Quick, fill it up at the sink.

Words to practice - Like, Five, Alike, Live, Kind

Ĕ

This is a short sound that will come out through your nose if you leave your tongue at the top of your mouth. This isn't good.

Lips are soft and round, and a little forward.

This sound has many spellings but it is still the same sound.

Many, leather, leisure, measure, treasure, head, again, Geoffrey, says. Note - the word 'says' is always and without exception pronounced 'sĕz'.

Sentences to practice:

- Many red hens are special
- He'll have a sore head again
- Let's measure the leather at your leisure
- Jenny sells eggs to Penny

Exercises for consonants.

Consonants are formed by two organs of articulation partially or completely contacting.

For example:

P and B are formed by the two lips contacting

T is produced by the tongue and teeth meeting

K, G, NG, is produced by the back of the tongue and soft palate meeting

There are 21 consonant letters in English but 30 consonant sounds, the following is a sample of the hardest sounds or the sounds that are usually not articulated correctly. If you want to learn all 30 consonant sounds in the Masterclass - Excellence in English book (also available on Amazon). To see all the exercises in video go to www.sayitclearly.co.nz or Miriam McKenzie YouTube.

SECTION ONE - Repeat the three you have chosen five times, getting faster and faster:

a) Lee Loo La

b) Pee Poo Pa

c) Dee Doo Da

d) Vee Voo Va

e) Ree Roo Ra

f) Flee Flu Fla

g) Tee Too Ta

SECTION TWO:

- Pass the pencils please, Paul
- Packing peppers posed problems
- Betty blew up the blue balloon
- Why will you worry when it is windy?
- Wanda watched the watermelon melting
- Wild wet wind wets the washing
- Which watch is the one you wanted?
- You always lose too many shoes
- Lots of hot coffee in a proper copper coffee pot

SECTION THREE:

- Will you leave the lazy lion alone?

- Will you wait for Winnie and Willie?

- Put the tip of the tongue to the top of the teeth

- Red leather: Yellow leather

- Red lorry: Yellow lorry

- A lump of red leather: a red leather lump

- Let's eat a lot of leeks

- Shall we shut the shop?

SECTION FOUR:

- I'm thinking of drinking some milk

- Bring your donging gong along

- Get a long length of string

- Go and get Gran's gift.

- I'm alone at home mending longs

- I think his drink is from the milk tank

- Birds sing in spring

- Garry plays the guitar and sings Go, Molly, Go.

- Gong – ong – ong – ong

- Giggle – Gaggle- Google

CHAPTER SEVEN - MODULATION

Choosing the right 'voice' to use in particular circumstances. Have you ever listened to a speaker and thought "Boring!" Chances are they only used one tone of voice without changing volume, pitch, pace or emphasising words, so that their speech was monotonous and boring. In this chapter, we will learn how to make your voice sound exciting when you are speaking aloud. W This will give you great confidence, not to mention high marks, when it comes to oral presentations at school, which we all have to do, in one form or another, as soon as (if not before) we start school.

Choose two exercises from each section.

Section One

Pitch - The height or depth of your voice

Repeat these words on one long breath, trying different pitches.

High pitch	Medium pitch	Low pitch

EXERCISE ONE

Drea...M	Drea...M	Drea...M
Moo...N	Moo...N	Moo...N
Boo...M	Boo...M	Boo...M

EXERCISE TWO

HOO	HOO	HOO
HOH	HOH	HOH
HAW	HAW	HAW
HAH	HAH	HAH
HAY	HAY	HAY
HEE	HEE	HEE

EXERCISE THREE

Repeat the same as above but round the other way, so you will start at the low pitch and then go higher.

Low pitch	Medium pitch	High pitch
HOO	HOO	HOO
HOH	HOH	HOH
HAW	HAW	HAW

HAH	HAH	HAH
HAY	HAY	HAY
HEE	HEE	HEE

4. Say each vowel sound as if you were asking a question.

A   E   I   O   U

5. Say each vowel sound as if you were giving an answer.

A   E   I   O   U

6. Say these sounds as different pitches. You choose whether high, medium or low.

EEE........OOO..........MMMM

Section Two

Pace - The speed at which we deliver our words

1. Count in threes, increasing pace with each group.

- 1,2,3
- 4,5,6
- 7,8,9
- 10,11,12
- 13,14,15

2. Do the same but with the alphabet.

- ABC
- DEF

- GHI
- JKL
- MNO
- PQR
- STU
- VWX
- YZ

3. Say these sentences three times each, getting faster and faster each time.

- Polly Parrot picked a pikelet
- Tommy turned the truck towards the truck

Section Three

Pause - A stop for breath, to create meaning and a sense of drama

There are many different types of pauses, but we usually know when to pause by punctuation like . , " " ? ! We must learn how to use pauses effectively so the audience can share our feelings.

Try these sentences below and pause when you see the -, then ask the person who is listening to you how it sounded. If you aren't sure how to pause, count two, three in your head, which will be a good starting point.

Once you get comfortable with pausing it will become easier and you will pause depending on how you sense the audience is reacting to you.

1. "I can't believe that you are doing this, - it is really hurting my feelings"

2. "Stop! – Stop! – You will break it, - if you don't"

3. "What did you think of that?- That was pretty cool, - wasn't it?"

4. "And then, - around the corner, - came this big, - scary, - hairy, - yellow-eyed monster! – I ran as fast as I could – to get away"

5. "Oh, - that was such a sad story, - tell another one"

Section Four

Emphasis and Inflection - The rise and fall of our voice

When we are reading we can see it's a question by the ? When we are listening to a speaker, we know they are asking a question by the rise in inflection in their voice at the end of the sentence.

1. Say each sentence three times and make your voice go faster, louder and higher each time, but make sure you

voice DOESN'T rise in inflection at the end of the sentence if is not a question.

Where are you?   Get out of here   What are you doing?

2. Say each sentence three times and make your voice go lower, slower and quieter each time.

Where are you?   Get out of here   What are you doing?

3. Say the words below in six different ways.   The different ways are:

Fast, loud, high, low, slow, quiet.

The words are:

"No" "Yes" "Well"

4. Ask the following sentence in these different ways - serious, surprised, angry, excited, shy.

"Are you coming by train?" (you will say this sentence five times in total)

Section Five

Tone - The richness of our voice

A person with nasal tone will sound whiny, a person with a hard, or harsh, tone will sound grumpy. These exercises will help you to get a tone of top quality, which will make people want to listen to your voice. We covered a lot of these exercises in the resonance chapter.

1. Start with a nice big yawn.

2. Keep that yawn feeling and say these sounds:

   MOO MOH MAW MAH MAY MEE

   NOO NOH NAW NAH NAY NEE

   NGOO   NGOH   NGAW   NGAHNGAY
       NGEE

3. Say these sounds: ah-ng-ah   oh-ng-oh   ee-ng-ee   ooh-ng-ooh aw-ng-aw   Ou-ng-ou

4. Say these words on one breath, three times - gloam, gleam, stream, dream

5. Hum this sound for as long as you can on one breath:

   MMMMMMMMMMMMMMMMMMMMMNNNNNNNNN
   NNNNNNNNNNNNNN

MMMMMMMMMMMMMMMMMMMMMNNNNNNNNN
NNNNNNNNNNNNNMMMMMMMMMMMMMM
MMMMMMNNNNNNNNNNNNNNNNNNNNN

6. Say these next sounds with your hand over your mouth on the M sound, and then take your hand away with the vowel sound.

MOO MOH MAW MAH MAY MEE

Section Six

Volume - How loudly or quietly we are speaking

Changing the volume of our voice makes people who are listening, listen more closely. It is a great tool to quieten your voice when telling an exciting part of your story and build the volume up as you get to the best bit.

1. Whisper as you count up to ten slowly, then repeat with a quiet voice, then speak it clearly, then as if speaking to a person across the room.

2. Hold your hand in front of your mouth about 15cm away and say "Hello, how are you?" Move your hand out so your arm is fully extended and repeat the sentence. Imagine someone is standing about 1 metre in front of you and say the sentence

again. Imagine someone is just outside the door and repeat the sentence. Imagine that someone is outside the gate and say the sentence again. This should be very loud but try not to shout, as this strains the voice.

3. Say the following sentences and you decide what volume your voice should be at: "Shhh, I'm trying to watch the movie"

"Look out! A car is coming!" "Are you looking for this? I found it over there"

"Hurry up, you're going to be late!"

"Look at that baby over there, she's asleep. How cute"

4. Say the alphabet and get louder as you get towards the end. Once again, don't shout as it will strain your voice.

5. Say the alphabet again, but this time start loud and get quieter and quieter as you go.

CHAPTER EIGHT - PROJECTION OR FORWARD PLACEMENT

Projecting your voice forward takes a lot of practice but is really necessary if you want your audience to hear you clearly and it is a very valuable tool. Of course, firstly make sure your neck and shoulder muscles are completely relaxed - choose two or three exercises from the relaxation chapter.

Start with the following, and then choose three or four exercises from each section, and have your children repeat after you.

Slowly unhinge your jaw and close again. MUST DO SLOWLY.

Chew like a cow, now like a rabbit

Yay - yay -yay-yay

Bah Bah Bah Bah

Busy brown bees, buzzing in the heather,

Brown bumble bees, humming altogether,

BBZZZZZZZZZZZZZZZZZZZZZZZZZZZZZZZ

HMMMMMMMMMMMMMMMMM

Walla Walla Bing Bang

Walla Walla ha!

Walla Walla Bing Bang

YO HO HO!

1. Whisper the following sounds.

   OO   OH   AW   AH   AY   EE

2. Whisper them again but hold the sound to the count of five.

3. Say these sounds and hold the M sound to the count of five.

   OO   OO   OO   MMMMMMMMMMMMMMMMM

   Repeat twice

4. Hum three short M sounds followed by one long M sound.

   M   M   M   MMMMMMMMMMMMMMMMM

   Repeat twice

5. Make the following sounds quietly and keep them going so they all run together.

   K.....AH....NG K.....AH....NG K....AH....NG

K....AH ....N   K....AH.....N   K.....AH....N

K....AH....M   K....AH.....M   K....AH...M

Open your mouth wide as if you are about to yawn. Say the sounds below while keeping the yawn feeling in your mouth. When you say the vowel, hear and feel the voice 'pop' off your lips with the B sound

BAH   BAH   BAH   BOO

BAH   BAH   BAH   BOH

BAH   BAH   BAH   BAW

BAH   BAH   BAH   BAY

BAH   BAH   BAH   BEE

6. Feel the lips vibrate with the M sound.

MAH   MAH   MAH   MOO

MAH   MAH   MAH   MOH

MAH   MAH   MAH   MAW

MAH   MAH   MAH   MAY

MAH   MAH   MAH   MEE

7. Say this on one tone, get faster and faster.

NG....AH.....NG....AH.....NG....AH....NG...AH....NG....AH

8. Say the word SH...AH as loudly as you can. Repeat two or three times. Now try the word VOO...ZEE

9. Keep saying these words over and over, feeling the vibration in the lips.

   Many many many many many many many many

   Mini mini mini mini mini mini mini mini mini mini

   Moan moan moan moan moan moan moan moan

10. Whisper the following sentences, then say them again with one tone, and then again in a normal speaking voice.

    Who are you

    We are three

    All hard law

    Slow past go

    May's last day

11. Hold your hand about 10cm away from your face and say "Ha ha ha" into your hand. Move your hand another 10cm and repeat, then another ten sentences and repeat. Keep repeating and imagine your voice carrying to the furthest away wall, then outside, then the back fence, over the road, to the neighbours.

12. Ask a person (imaginary if you need) beside you "How are you?" Now imagine they are at the door as you say it, then by the mailbox, then over the road.

13. Whisper "Hello, can I help you?" so everyone in the room can hear you.

14. You will need a partner for this. Stand facing a wall and the other person facing another wall. Now have a conversation with each other and not looking at each other.

15. Select an object in the room that is a distance from you. Point at it and then as you take a deep breath in, draw your arm back over your shoulder. Then throw that arm back to the object you chose and at the same time ask these questions. Do it one at a time and emphasise the last word.

"Do it NOW"

"Don't touch that BUTTON"

"Where are you going NOW?"

"You forgot your KEY!"

"Look out, look OUT"

CHAPTER NINE - INDISTINCT SPEECH

Does your suffer from mumble-itis, or do you think you're Speedy Gonzalez, and the quicker you speak the faster you will get the job done?

If you want to correct the 'mumble' or speak too quickly when speaking or reading aloud, make up a lesson of the following.

1. Exercises from the relaxation chapter

2. Exercises from the breathing chapter

3. Exercises from the consonants section of the articulation chapter

4. These following exercises (the tongue exercises might provide some humour – they do look funny).

   a. Stretch your lower lip over your upper teeth. Stretch the upper lip over your lower teeth. Keep doing this getting faster and faster.

b. Pucker your lips up as if to kiss someone, then stretch them as widely as possible. Do this ten times as fast as you can.

c. Itch the roof of your mouth with the tip of your tongue. Do this five times.

d. Push your tongue hard into one cheek and then the other. Try to touch your nose with your tongue, chin, one ear then the other.

e. Push your tongue out of your mouth as far as possible then let it relax. Do this five times.

f. Press your whole tongue against the roof of your mouth and relax. Repeat five times.

CHAPTER TEN – FIXING OTHER SPEECH FAULTS

These exercises may help in fixing a speech fault, however, if you have any concerns about a physiological or physical problem, please contact your doctor or consult a speech language therapist.

Speech depends on consonants for distinctness and clarity.

As you have been practising consonant sounds in every other chapter of this book, without probably knowing it, included in this section are only five consonant sounds to practise.

These sounds are S, L, Th, R and T when it is heard at the end of a word.

When children are learning to speak, S, L and TH can be some of the last sounds they learn and may need extra practise if they are five or six and still working on saying these sounds correctly. If you have concerns about these (or any other sounds) that your children have difficulty producing, you may want to see your doctor or a speech language therapist.

S

The sides of your tongue should touch the ridges of your upper teeth. Make sure your tongue tip is not through the teeth (this will make the TH sound). Tongue tip should be down. Try blowing air down a drinking straw – note the air goes between the two top and bottom teeth so if these are missing this sound might be a bit difficult. Wait for your second teeth to come for this sound.

- Say this poem to practise:
- Send the sound
- In a little hiss
- Lips quite round
- And teeth like this.
- The sides of tongue
- You firmly press
- On your side teeth
- And there's an S!

L

Look in the mirror for this one because where the L is in a word will change what your tongue is going to do. Relax your jaw, tongue tip behind your top teeth, and say: lah, lah, lah. Now say loo, loo, loo. For loo loo loo, the tip of your tongue will touch the roof of your mouth just behind your teeth.

b

- Try these in the order you see them:
- Lash, clash, flag
- Little, bottle, brittle
- Field, held, hold.

In the verse below make you the L is heard in milk. Keep the tongue tip pressed up to the back of the top teeth for this sound. There are more exercises in Chapter Ten for this L sound (when in words like 'milk' it's called a dark L).

TH

Put your tongue tip softly between your front teeth when making this sound. Practise it now.

TH TH TH TH TH TH TH THTHTHTHTH

Say these sentences:

1. Arthur thanked Martha for thumping the thing with all her strength.
2. The toothpaste and toothbrush were in the third bathroom.
3. The width and breadth of the baths were beneath Jonathan's oath.
4. Theo thrilled Faith on Thursday with a thousand songs.
5. Three moths flew down the path.

6. In the theatre the theology students thudded through the filthy throng.

7. Mother and Father thought they could trust Ethel with the fourth thimble.

R

Curl the tip of your tongue near the roof of your mouth and blow air through to shake it. It should make a sound like a lawnmower (kind of). Keep practising until you can make a long sound (listening to the audio will help). If this is difficult, there are exercises in chapter ten to help.

Choose two or three sentences at a time for practise:

1. Rachel runs round red rectangles.

2. Rascals ran rapidly round Robin's rocket recently.

3. Greedy Gertrude grabbed Grandma's grapes.

4. Grandpa drenched the drum.

5. The stream gurgled through rocks and crops.

6. won:run   will:rill   wake:rake   wince:rinse

    wound:round   way:ray   war:roar

    woe:row   wise:rise   wink:rink

7. Hurry Harry to the road before the lorry comes.

8. Look up the tree to see the trick Ronda is playing with the trumpet.

9. The thirsty ground soaks up the drops.

10. The drama produced by the graduates was all rather merry.

T

One of the worst sounds we are hearing on the radio and TV today is the 't' at the end of words that end with this letter. It is not being enunciated! The 't' is NOT silent and it should be heard (same with D for that matter) when it is at the end of a word. Listen to my audio for examples and you will understand why this sounds so sloppy and lazy.

T and D are partners. Bring the tip of the tongue to the centre of your top teeth and quickly move it down. You will be able to hear a very quiet T/D sound without actually using breath.

MAKE SURE YOU MAKE A 'T' SOUND AT THE END OF THE WORDS THAT HAVE A 'T' AT THE END!!

Practise:

1. The cat sat on the mat.

2. He said to cut the tap off the pipe.

3. Put the television on the table.

4. Shut the door tightly.

5. Naughty Tina tied the cat to the trunk of a tree.

6. Left on the street was a terrified tiny troll.

7. Take a tour this winter to see the tigers.

8. Ten tiny tinkers taking tea.

9. Terrible tiresome Tuesdays.

10. Terry Turtle tickled Tim terribly.

SUBSTITUTION OF SOUNDS.

1. Saying the W sound instead of R. For example, Wobert instead of Robert.

To correct this:

The teeth must be apart.

The back of the tongue must not rise to touch the top of the mouth.

The tip of the tongue must curl back into the mouth but not touch teeth, gums or roof of mouth.

For flexibility of the tongue practise these:.

IIL   IIL   IIL   IIL - start slow, then build up speed, then slow down.

SH IIIL SH IIIL   SH IIIL SH IIIIL

T SH SH SH   T SH SH SH   T SH SH SH   T SH SH SH

SH SH SH T   SH SH SH T   SH SH SH T   SH SH SH T

SH ER OO   SH ER AW   SH ER AH   SH ER AY   SH ER

EE

Say a long ER sound, at the same time curling the tongue behind the gum ridge, and then make sure the tongue tip is behind the lower teeth for the vowel sound.

ER R OO ER R OH ER R AW ER R AH ER R AY

ER R EEE

Practise these words and sentences.

Red   rule   round   river   runs   really   very   brown

Bring three lorries round to the front

The long red river runs round the bend

Substituting the TH sound.

To pronounce the TH sound, follow the instructions above and use these to practise:

Keeping the teeth apart, hold the tip of the tongue very lightly against the upper front teeth. Blow air through the tongue in short, sharp puffs.

Say the following sounds, making sure the tongue moves into the TH position slowly.

OOTHOO	OHTHOH	AWTHAW
AHTHAH	AYTHAY	EETHEE

One common substitution of the TH sound is with the F sound. With this common mispronunciation the person would say 'Fank you' instead of 'thank you'.

To correct this - Do not bite your lower lip when they are saying or reading the TH sound. You must put your tongue between your teeth for this sound. Look in the mirror to see the difference.

2. Substituting W for L - Instead of saying 'lolly' they would say 'wolly', or instead of 'like' you would say 'yike'.

The tip of the tongue must touch the gum ridge in behind the front teeth, instead of lying flat for the W sound.

Practise:

la la la la la la, ensure you are getting the correct sound and the tongue is in the correct position. Do this in a mirror.

Lee lee lee lee lee

OOLI   OHLI AWLI AHLI AYLI EELI

Leave the lazy lion alone

The letter is lost

A little less likely

3. Dark L is the L sound in words like 'milk' and it is usually the vowel sound before the L that is enunciated, making it sound as if there isn't an L in the word at all.

Practise:

OOOO   OO   OO   OO   OO

OOL   OOL OOL OOL OOL

OOLG   OOLG OOLG OOLG OOLG

OOLK   OOLK OOLK OOLK OOLK

OOLG   OHLG AWLG AHLG AYLG EELG

OOLK   OHLK AWLK AHLK AYLK EELK

Words to practise

Milk, kettle, little, silly, chilly, fellow, bottle, killed, silk, gold, sulk, healed, mauled.

I sincerely hope you use this manual on a regular basis. If you wish to see changes in how your child speaks, it is very important to practise over and over.

Good luck and I look forward to hearing your feedback so please leave a review!

To see all the explanations and exercises in video go to www.sayitclearly.co.nz or Miriam McKenzie YouTube.

Miriam McKenzie

B.Ed, Dip. Tchg, ATCL (Practical Speech and Drama)

Made in the USA
Coppell, TX
04 July 2025

51484582R00039